AF270215

Cuckoo Wasp

by Grace Hansen

Abdo Kids Jumbo is an Imprint of Abdo Kids
abdobooks.com

abdobooks.com

Published by Abdo Kids, a division of ABDO, P.O. Box 398166, Minneapolis, Minnesota 55439.
Copyright © 2022 by Abdo Consulting Group, Inc. International copyrights reserved in all countries.
No part of this book may be reproduced in any form without written permission from the publisher.
Abdo Kids Jumbo™ is a trademark and logo of Abdo Kids.

Printed in the United States of America, North Mankato, Minnesota.

052021

092021

THIS BOOK CONTAINS
RECYCLED MATERIALS

Photo Credits: Alamy, iStock, Science Source, Shutterstock

Production Contributors: Teddy Borth, Jennie Forsberg, Grace Hansen
Design Contributors: Candice Keimig, Victoria Bates

Library of Congress Control Number: 2020947654
Publisher's Cataloging-in-Publication Data

Names: Hansen, Grace, author.

Title: Cuckoo wasp / by Grace Hansen

Description: Minneapolis, Minnesota : Abdo Kids, 2022 | Series: Incredible insects | Includes online
    resources and index.

Identifiers: ISBN 9781098207366 (lib. bdg.) | ISBN 9781644945568 (pbk.) | ISBN 9781098208202
    (ebook) | ISBN 9781098208622 (Read-to-Me ebook)

Subjects: LCSH: Chrysididae--Juvenile literature. | Wasps--Juvenile literature. | Desert animals--Juvenile
    literature. | Insects--Juvenile literature. | Insects--Behavior--Juvenile literature.

Classification: DDC 595.7--dc23

Table of Contents

Cuckoo Wasps

Cuckoo Wasps can be found in many countries throughout the world. They prefer warm, dry places.

These insects are quite small.

They grow to be just a half inch

(1.27 cm) in length.

Cuckoo wasps are sometimes

called emerald or jewel wasps.

This is because of their amazing

metallic and colorful bodies.

9

Cuckoo wasps are usually green or blue in color. But they can also be red and gold.

Acting Cuckoo

Cuckoo wasps are named after cuckoo birds. *Cuckoo* is a word meaning "silly" or "crazy." Cuckoos lay their eggs in other birds' nests. Another bird cares for the chick after it hatches.

marsh warbler bird
cuckoo chick
13

Cuckoo wasps lay their eggs in other insects' nests too. They do this in order to feed their own young.

Female cuckoo wasps fly until they find a bee or wasp nest. They must sneak carefully into the nest. Then they lay their eggs.

When the eggs hatch, the

cuckoo wasp **larvae** have lots

to eat. They feed on the eggs

and larvae of the bees or wasps

in the nest.

The cuckoo wasp **larvae** eat and grow. Then they become **pupae**. When the wasps become adults they leave the nest. They go in search of **mates**.

More Facts

- Cuckoo wasps that are gold or reddish in color are called "gold wasps" or "ruby wasps."

- Cuckoo wasps are often caught trying to sneak into other insects' nests. Other wasps and bees will grab the invader and throw it out of the nest.

- Cuckoo wasps have a good defense for when they get caught. They tuck their legs in and roll themselves into a ball. This makes it harder for other insects to grab or harm them.

Glossary

larva – an insect after it hatches from an egg and before it changes into its adult form. A larva does not have any wings and looks like a worm.

metallic – having reflective properties and colors that seem to change at different angles.

mate – one of a pair of insects that have young together.

pupa – an inactive insect; the stage between larva and adult.

Index

Abdo Kids ONLINE
FREE! ONLINE MULTIMEDIA RESOURCES

Visit abdokids.com to access crafts, games, videos, and more!

Use Abdo Kids code ICK7366 or scan this QR code!